Looking Good

SKIN

by Arlene C. Rourke

Rourke Publications, Inc.
Vero Beach, FL 32964

The author wishes to thank the following people for their help in the preparation of this book:

Dixie Montegomery, owner and director of a modeling school and agency.

Eileen Griffin, artist, illustrator and owner of a graphic arts company.

A special thanks to **Dr. John W. McDonald** for his professional advice. Dr. McDonald is a dermatologist practicing in Florida.

© 1987 Rourke Publications, Inc.

Library of Congress Cataloging in Publication Data

Rourke, Arlene, 1944-
   Skin.

   Bibliography: p.
   Includes index.
   Summary: Explains how to take care of the skin,
from cleaning to using make-up.
   1. Skin—Care and hygiene—Juvenile literature.
   2. Beauty, Personal—Juvenile literature.   [1. Skin—
Care and hygiene.   2. Beauty, Personal]   I. Title.
RL87.R85   1986   646.7'26   86-10093
ISBN 0-86625-276-2

CONTENTS

SKIN

Do you know that your skin is the largest organ in your body? On the average, one square inch of skin contains:

94 oil glands
19 feet of blood vessels
625 sweat glands
19,000,000 cells

Human skin varies in thickness. The skin around your eyes is much thinner and more delicate than the skin on the bottom of your feet.

Skin is divided into two main layers.
> The *dermis* is the inner section. It is made up of healthy, living cells.
> The *epidermis* is the outer section. The uppermost layer is the part that you see. It is made up of old, dead cells that are constantly being worn off.

The drawing on the opposite page shows you how the skin works. *Nerve endings* give you your sense of touch. Hair grows out of tubes called *follicles*. *Sweat glands* lying deep in the skin send out waste through the *pores*. *Oil glands* produce a substance called *sebum*, which keeps the skin and hair soft and flexible.

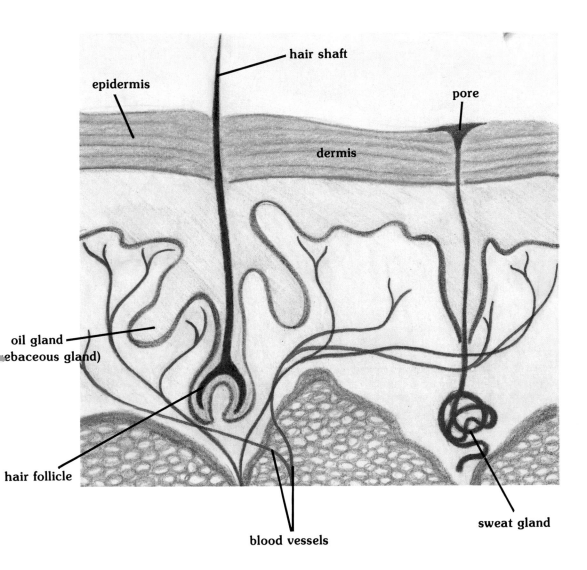

hair shaft

epidermis

pore

dermis

oil gland
(sebaceous gland)

hair follicle

blood vessels

sweat gland

5

Good, healthy skin has open pores. Body oil and sweat are constantly being released. The epidermis sheds its dead cells, and new, living ones come up from the dermis. When this balance is maintained, your skin looks and feels smooth and clear.

What Is Your Skin Type?

Ideal skin is neither oily nor dry. It is evenly colored. It has small pores and excellent texture. It never develops pimples or blackheads. It is not affected by changes in diet or climate. It is easily cared for with soap and water. It requires almost no makeup.

What? You don't have ideal skin? Relax! Almost no one does.

There are three basic types of skin: *dry*, *oily*, and *combination*. Almost all of us fall into one of these types. How you care for your skin and the products you use on it will be determined by your skin type. To identify the type of skin you have, first study your skin carefully.

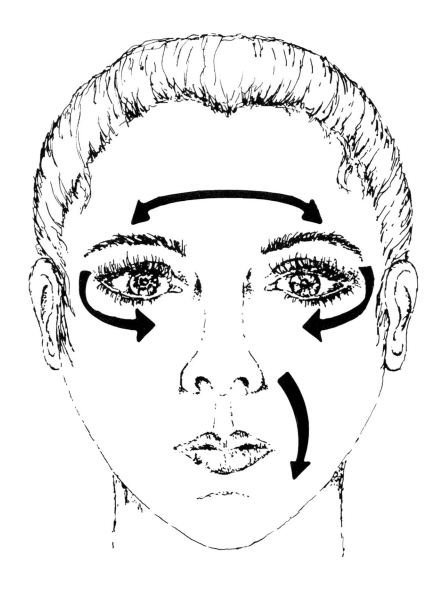

Skin Type A: Is your skin dry, flaky, thin, and tight, especially after washing? Do extreme changes in relative humidity affect your skin? Do you burn easily in the sun?

You have *dry skin*.

7

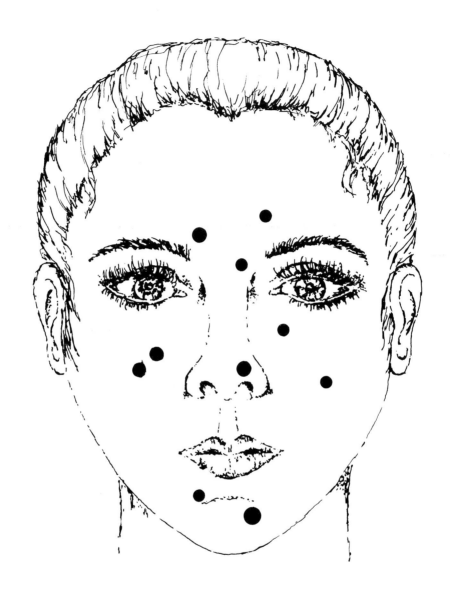

Skin Type B: Is your skin shiny, greasy, and coarse? Do you have large pores? Do you get a lot of pimples and blackheads?

You have *oily skin*.

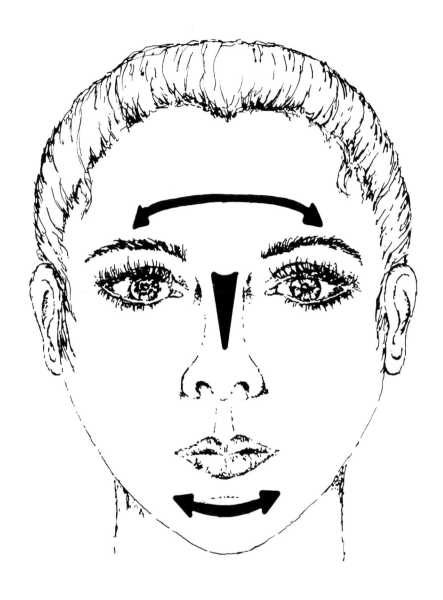

Skin Type C: Is your skin dry on the cheeks and near the hairline, but oily on the forehead, nose, and chin?

You have *combination skin*.

CLEANLINESS

Skin care is one of the most important aspects of looking good. You will look and feel better if your skin is healthy and glowing.

We know that very few people have ideal skin. So don't be disappointed if your skin is less than perfect. Even beautiful models and actresses have problems with their skin. However, they recognize their problems and know how to care for their skin. They make the effort. You can, too.

The Tools

Soaps and cleansers Keeping your skin clean is the most important part of skin care. There are many types of soaps and cleansers on the market. Use one that suits your skin type. If you have dry skin, *always* use a mild soap or cleanser. Ask your druggest or cosmetician for the name of a good superfatted soap or a moisturizing cleanser. Superfatted soaps have a natural moisturizer in them. After using the product, take the time to wash it off thoroughly. Soap or cleanser left on the skin can be very drying. If you have dry skin avoid using hot water.

If you have oily skin, you may think that using a harsh soap or very astringent (drying) cleanser will dry up your excess oil. Actually, those products will probably irritate your skin even more. A good, mild soap, used a few times a day, will be more effective.

Moisturizers   Every day your skin loses water. In order to keep your skin soft, you have to replace that water. Moisturizers are light, non-greasy lotions which are used to soften the skin and prevent dryness. Drinking water and using a good moisturizer help the skin keep a good water balance. If you have dry skin, you will need to use moisturizer often.

TIP: Here's a good way of getting the most out of your moisturizer: After washing your face, while the skin is still wet, apply a thin film of moisturizer. You will have the double benefit of water and moisturizer.

Make-up removers   If you wear make-up you will find it easier to clean your face with special make-up removers. Mascara can be very difficult to get off. A good eye make-up remover will be a great help. Avoid alcohol based products.

Masque   Masques come in gel or paste form. Use them to clean the pores and slough off the dead skin. Always avoid the eye area. Read and follow the package directions carefully! Don't leave the masque on longer than recommended. It can really dry out your skin.

TIP: Masques can be very expensive. You might want to try using a homemade masque.

Here are recipes for two masques that are easy to prepare and cost just pennies:

For dry skin:

Mix together two tablespoons of almond oil and two tablespoons of honey. Heat until it is just lukewarm. Do not let it get hot! Apply to face with fingers. Let cool. Rinse off with lukewarm water. Use a moisturizer afterward.

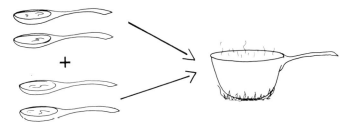

For oily skin:

Mix one cup of raw oatmeal with enough water to make a paste. Apply to face. Let dry. Rinse with warm water.

Water Water is not generally thought of as a beauty product, but water can do more for you than most expensive cosmetics. Water aids circulation, and it carries nutrients to all parts of the body. It regulates body temperature and cleanses the body of waste materials. Drink between six and eight glasses of water a day in order to get all the benefits that water can give you.

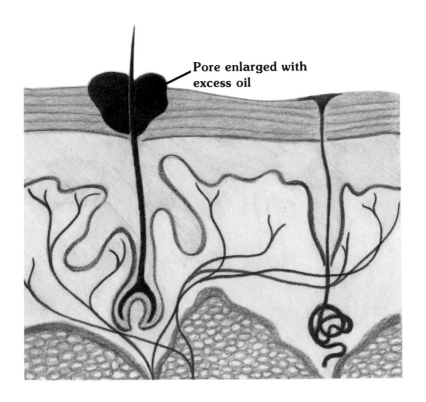

Pore enlarged with excess oil

Acne

Pimples, usually on the face, are called *acne*. During adolescence, the glands increase their output of oil and sebum. Sometimes the pores are not able to release all that excess oil. It becomes trapped. Bacteria invades. The result is pimples.

Most teenagers get acne at one time or another. It is usually a minor problem and disappears by the early twenties. Cleanliness will help control your acne problem.

Some teenagers have severe acne. It is painful and embarassing. Unless it is properly treated, it can lead to permanent scarring. If you think that you have a severe case of acne, you should see a doctor who is a skin specialist, called a dermatolotist. There is no single "cure" for acne, but the doctor will advise you on the treatment that is right for you.

Guidelines for Healthy Skin

Keep it clean! Cleanliness is the basis of beauty. Wash your face twice a day, or more often if you have oily skin. Shampoo twice a week, or more often if you have an oily scalp.

Drink six to eight glasses of water a day. Sodas don't count as water.

Eat a balanced diet. Go easy on the fats and high calorie foods.

Get plenty of sleep. Your body is growing and needs time to restore itself.

Get plenty of exercise. It's good for circulation and it burns up calories.

Use a sunblock.

Keep your hands away from your face. We all have the habit of playing with our hair or face. Hands carry many germs which can be spread to the face.

If you have acne, everything above applies to you, plus:

No matter how great the temptation, *don't squeeze those pimples!* Squeezing causes them to spread, and you could get a bad infection.

Avoid wearing heavy, greasy make-up. Make-up traps the bacteria on your skin. Your pores need air. Use oil-free make-up.

The Sun and Your Health

Medical science has absolute proof that too much sun is dangerous to your health! Continual sun exposure can cause skin cancer and premature aging of the skin.

Sunburn is a painful condition caused by over-exposure to the sun. These suggestions will help prevent sunburn:

Avoid sun exposure between 10 A.M. and 2 P.M. when the sun's rays are the strongest.

Wear a sun hat or a visor if your face burns easily. Wear a good beach cover-up.

If you do want to get a tan, allow only fifteen minutes for the first day, and increase exposure gradually.

Pool, lake, and ocean water all reflect and intensify the sun's rays. Sand and snow have the same effect.

Sunblocks help protect the skin from the sun's ultraviolet (burning) rays. Some blocks are water resistant; others are not. If you swim, you will need a block that is water resistant.

Sunblocks come in different SPF (blocking) ratings. If you are fair-skinned, you probably need the highest SPF number. Read package directions carefully.

TIP: Contrary to popular belief, dark-skinned people do burn. However, you might want to use a lower SPF block than fair-skinned people do.

GETTING TO KNOW YOURSELF

In this chapter, you will learn how to identify your face shape. The ideal face shape is the oval shape. As with ideal skin, almost no one has a perfectly oval face. As you grow older and begin using make-up, the shape of your face will be a factor in determining what type of make-up you will use and where you will apply it.

OVAL FACE

ROUND FACE

SQUARE FACE

TRIANGULAR FACE

MAKE-UP

Ask your parents for permission when you feel that you are ready to begin using make-up.

If they agree, start experimenting carefully. The two worst mistakes that girls and women make when applying make-up is using too much and using it in the wrong places. Cosmetic application is an art. Every line and dab should have a reason for being there. You probably don't need as much make-up as you think you do. When in doubt, leave it out!

How to Begin

Study your face. What are your good features? With what features are you not so happy? You will want to play up your best features and tone down the less-than-lovely ones.

Do you have great eyes? Are they a pretty color? Learn how to make them up so that they are your most important feature.

Do you have clear, evenly colored skin? You may not need foundation or concealer. Just a little powder will keep the shine down.

TIP: Cosmetics can be very expensive. Start using a few slowly until you get a feel for what you need.

20

The Tools

Generally, young people don't have a lot of money to spend on make-up. Unless you really want an expensive, name-brand cosmetic, the same effect can be achieved with a less expensive brand.

One of the few exceptions to that rule involves the selection of make-up brushes. Good make-up brushes are an absolute must if you are going to apply make-up correctly. Buy sable brushes. They are the best. They are expensive, but they will last a long time with good care.

Concealer helps hide blemishes and black circles under the eyes. Choose a shade as close to your skin type as possible. A concealer that is too white under your eyes will make you look ghostly.

Foundation evens out uneven coloring. Again, choose a shade that matches your skin tone. Avoid shades that are too "pinky." They tend to look phony. If you have dry skin, try an oil-based foundation. People with oily skin would benefit from a water-based foundation.

Powder should be applied with a powder brush. Powder puffs tend to give you a chalky look, and they carry a lot of germs. Use powder to eliminate shine. For that purpose, you need translucent powder.

Eye shadow can be a marvelous enhancer. Don't try to match your eye shadow to your outfit. Instead, choose a color that really makes your eyes look pretty. Powder shadows tend to stay on longer. Also, they don't settle in the creases.

Eye liner is used around the outer side of the eyelashes. It makes the eyes appear to be larger. The key words when applying liner are, *"Go easy!"* Nothing is phonier than Cleopatra eyes. For most girls, a medium brown shade is best. Unless you have black skin, don't use black liner.

Mascara gives the impression that eyelashes are longer and fuller. As with eye liner, brown is best for most girls.

Blusher is used to give the skin a nice, healthy glow. Peaches and clear pinks look best on fair skins. Olive-skinned people find that bright, clear reds complement their color. If you have black skin, try a reddish-coral blusher to add a little pizzaz!

Lipstick is your last, but not least important, make-up item. Follow the same color suggestions as with blushes. You redheads have to be especially careful in choosing a lip color. The wrong shade of pink can look awful. Stick to clear reds, russets, and burnt oranges.

Common Sense Suggestions

Make-up must be removed at the end of the day. Give your skin a chance to breathe at night.

Never let anyone borrow your make-up. Germs are easily spread when make-up is passed around.

If you are using cake eyeliner, wet it with water. Don't spit in it.

If you wear contact lenses, ask your doctor if you should put them in before or after applying eye make-up.

If you wear contact lenses, always close your eyes when spraying perfume, hair spray, or spray deodorant.

Wash make-up brushes every few days. Wash sponges after each use. Use a mild soap and rinse thoroughly.

HOW TO APPLY MAKE-UP

Start with a clean face.

Be sure the lighting is good.

Apply moisturizer, if you are using one, about ten minutes before you start making up.

Apply concealer after moisturizer is absorbed.

TIP: Don't get discouraged if your first efforts don't turn out well. Good make-up application requires practice and patience.

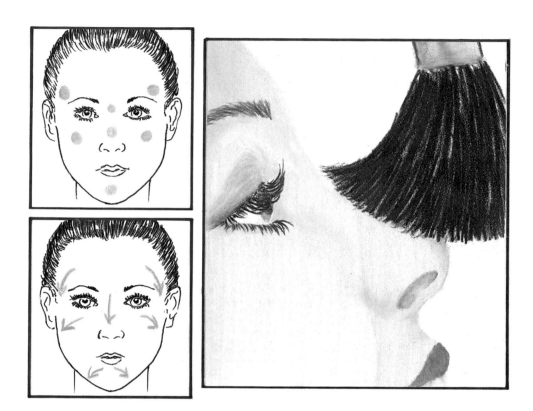

First, dot foundation over your face.

Next, blend it with fingers or a cosmetic sponge in the directions show.

Then, apply translucent powder with a powder brush.

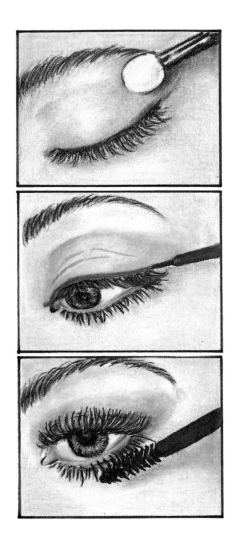

First, apply *eye* shadow, as shown.

Next, apply a *thin* line of *eye* liner to the outer corners of the upper and lower lids. Smudge it for a more natural look.

Last, apply mascara: Look down. Starting at the roots, apply to the top of the upper lashes. Look up. Apply to the underside.

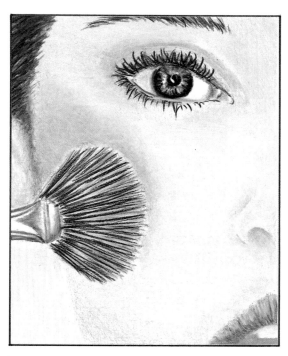

Apply blusher over the cheekbone moving upward and outward to the temples.

TIP: To slim down round cheeks, apply blusher *below* the cheekbone and upward toward the center of the ear.

First, apply foundation to your lips.

Then, following the natural line of your lips, apply the lipstick. Tinted gloss gives a more natural look.

TIP: Try using a lip pencil to line your lips before applying lipstick. Lip pencil will give you a better lip line.

BIBLIOGRAPHY

Skin Care and Makeup Book, Christine Valmy. Crown Publishers, Inc., New York.

The Skin Care Book, Arnold W. Klein, M.D., James H. Sternberg, M.D. and Paul Bernstein. Collier Books, division of Macmillan, New York.

The Good Looks Skin Book, Sarah R. Riedman, PhD. Julian Messner, a division of Simon and Schuster, New York.

Vogue Beauty, Deborah Hutton. Harmony Books, New York.

Designing Your Face, Way Bandy. Random House, New York.

The Art of Being Beautiful, Bedford Shelmire, Jr., M.D. St. Martin's Press, New York.

Super Skin, Jonathan Zizmor, M.D. and John Foreman. Thomas Crowell Company, New York.

Newsweek Magazine. June 9, 1986, pps. 60-69.

About Face, Jeffrey Bruce and Sherry Suib Cohen. G.P. Putman's Sons, New York.

Dry Skin and Common Sense, Dale Alexander. Witkower Press, Inc., West Hartford, Connecticut.

TLC for Summer Skin, Woman's Day. July 13, 1982 pps 88-90.

Suntans and Skin Cancer, Newsweek Magazine. June 14, 1982, p. 85.

"Coming Clean," Seventeen. January 1986. p. 76.

"All About Problem Skin," Seventeen. March 1985, p. 113.

"Sun and Skin," Seventeen. June 1985, p. 38.

INDEX